The Fan

King Loofah

Rhian Baker

Illustrated by Jan Nesbitt

Ginn

The beginning

Loofah was (and for all I know, still is) king of a great and beautiful island, "The Island Out at Sea". The island was covered in trees that blossomed with diamonds and all sorts of delicious fruit. There were streams with bridges, cascading waterfalls and birds of every colour and tune. Swirls of pink and starry mist surrounded and protected the island. King Loofah loved his island kingdom. He was a happy man and a kind ruler.

And, up until the time this story takes place, King Loofah was just an ordinary sort of king. He made a few rules, gave yearly garden parties, opened fêtes and schools, smashed bottles of champagne over new ships and generally did the things kings do. But then something happened to King Loofah, and he was never the same again.

How King Loofah is swallowed by a Sea-Serpent

One night there was a terrible storm. It was so fierce that the waves rattled and shook the island until Loofah was thrown out of his peaceful dreams and comfortable bed. Grumbling royally, he pulled his trousers up over his pyjamas and put on his furry coat and crown. Then he went down to the shore to inspect the damage. As he stooped down to empty the water from one of his boots (a little fish had swum in and Loofah could feel it tickling his toes), a giant wave, mean and grey-looking, crashed and thundered onto the beach.

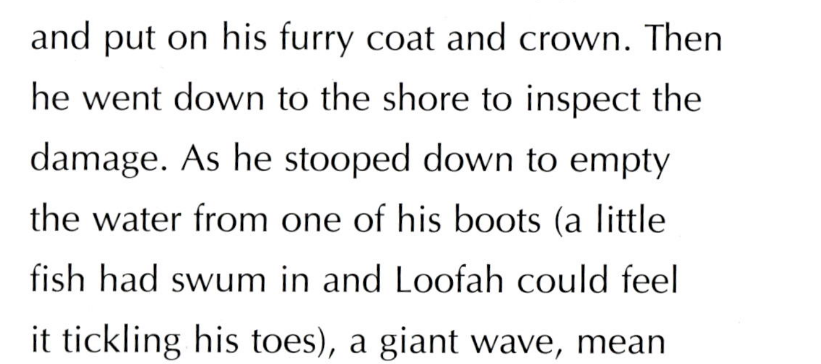

Suddenly, before the poor king could run to safety, the giant wave had tossed and ducked him into the sea. With a wicked chuckle, the wave kicked Loofah into the huge and horrid mouth of a waiting Sea-Serpent.

"GOAL!" King Loofah heard the other waves yelling as he disappeared into the long dark cave of the Serpent's stomach.

Inside the Serpent's stomach and how King Loofah escapes

Although Loofah was rather stunned and very bruised, he felt there was no time to waste. He would have to explore the stomach and then plan his escape. He wished he had brought his camera. After a bit of fumbling about, he was relieved to find that at least his notebook and pencil were still in his pyjama pocket. (It is said that all kings take notebooks to bed, in case of late-night brainwaves.) Although the notebook and pencil were extremely soggy, they were still of use.

Loofah wrote down:

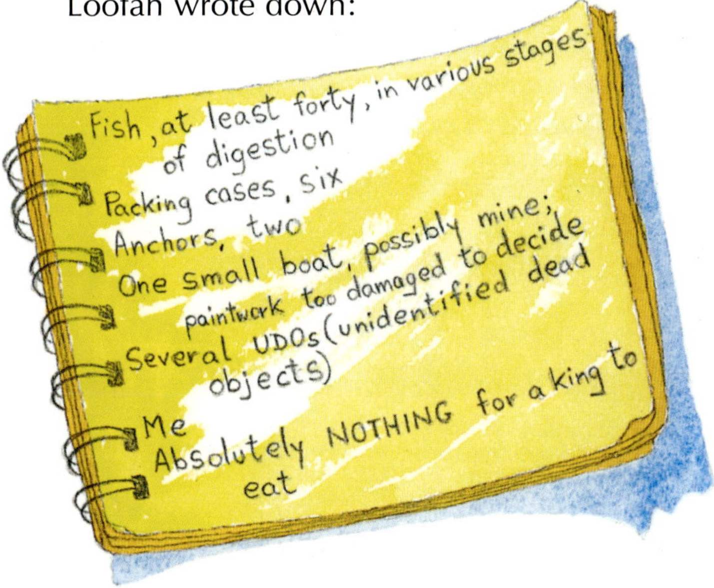

This was the list of things he found in the stomach, and King Loofah decided this was probably a fairly ordinary sort of Serpent, and that he would be quite safe, for the moment. Looking around more carefully, he realised that planning his escape was not going to be easy.

The entire cave was covered in a thick, slimy skin, and there appeared to be no beginning or end to it, so large was the creature. It was also very dark and incredibly smelly—not at all like home, thought Loofah. He had only the fish to keep him company and soon Loofah began to feel rather miserable.

He couldn't think of even one good idea for escaping. This was very unusual for Loofah, since he was always having terrific ideas at home, about parties for children, and different ways of slaying dragons, and new and fantastic flavours for ice-cream. But this ... this was something altogether quite different. He sat down in the boat and, for a while, tried not to think at all. (He was taking his own advice by doing this. It was something he often told other kings, who envied his quick and clever mind, to do.)

It worked! An idea came.

"Oh, helloooo, Serpent, dear friend!" he shouted. "Let me out of here, there's a kind fellow!"

No answer.

Loofah tried again. "Serpent, listen! Let me out of here and I will make you king. I will make you king of everything you can see from the Palace Window!"

Loofah thought he heard a faint rumbling from somewhere very far above, or maybe far below, it was really too hard to say. Then, suddenly, a great ball of water thundered out of nowhere, knocking Loofah straight off his feet. The next thing he knew was that he had been spat out of the miserable cave and was bobbing about in the water, under the Serpent's terrible stare.

"Sssplendid idea, little King," hissed the Serpent. "But I want a crown to wear right now," he added, "or else, no deal!"

Luckily, King Loofah had a spare crown in the pocket of his furry coat (where all kings keep their spares, in case you didn't know) and, after giving it a quick polish with his sleeve, he held it up to the Serpent's gaze.

"Yesss, all right, it'll do for now," the Serpent said, rather ungratefully, Loofah thought. "Put it on my head, here between the two hornsss."

The Serpent bent his head closer to the king's outstretched arms, until Loofah was able to place the crown on the green, slimy head. He wedged it tightly between the two dangerously sharp, spear-like horns.

Loofah then climbed up the Serpent's neck, slipping and sliding, until eventually he managed to seat himself just behind its head. Removing the cord from his pyjama bottoms, he tied himself to one of the great horns. The Serpent complained a lot, and Loofah had to keep reminding him that if he didn't return them to the island, then he couldn't possibly make him a king. And so, at last, tired King Loofah and the Serpent headed for home.

How King Loofah meets Neptune and gets to ride in a parachute

Their progress was very slow because the Serpent kept stopping every five minutes to show off his crown to whatever sea-creature passed them. And the sea was particularly busy, with everyone clearing up after the storm.

So King Loofah and the Serpent hadn't gone very far when, just in front of them, appeared some sort of whirlpool, with the waves around it frothing and foaming. The waves rose higher and higher until they began to sway apart, leaving a hole right down to the bottom of the sea, as if someone had pulled out the plug.

"Oh well, at least I'll be able to walk home now," thought Loofah, who was extremely uncomfortable sitting on the Serpent's spiny neck.

From out of the gap in the waves, there appeared the head of the largest man Loofah had ever seen, a giant giant, with a long, long beard of seaweed and little fish, and a nose the size of a sack of gold, all covered in barnacles and mussels. As he stood up to his full height, his sandy head reached the clouds, and his eyes stared straight down at Loofah.

Very slowly the giant picked up the trembling king and lifted him to his face. Loofah gasped bravely as he watched the world become smaller and smaller, and the blue eyes and tremendous nose loom closer and closer.

"And which little King are you?" boomed the mighty man, blasting Loofah with sea-salt breath, and pointing to his best crown. Loofah decided he would handle this rather rude person in his most kingly manner—polite but firm.

"I am King Loofah, king of the most beautiful and rich island, where only the nicest people live. I am taking the Serpent back to my Palace, and plan to make him king of all he can see through my Palace Window. Allow us to continue on our way, there's a good man, and I can make you a king too!"

The giant man listened, and then roared with laughter, which almost deafened Loofah. "You little midget! Make me a king?" He lifted the crown off Loofah's head. "But I am already a king, a great king with all the riches I could ever want. I am Neptune, king of the deep, blue and sometimes green sea!" He placed Loofah's crown on his little finger, and held it up to the sun, where it shone and glittered. "But in exchange for this little trinket, I shall let you and your Serpent friend pass."

Loofah thought he'd never met such a cheeky person in all his life. While he fumed and raged quietly to himself, the King of the Sea rummaged in his pocket, and took out a large handkerchief, embroidered with singing mermaids. This he tied onto the braces of Loofah's trousers and then, holding Loofah's left foot between his enormous finger and thumb, he held him out over the sea … and let him go!

Loofah found himself floating down towards the Serpent. The handkerchief above him was filled with air and looked like a giant's umbrella. "If only my people could see me now," thought the airborne king, "how proud of me they would be. 'Is there no end to his talents?' they would say."

BUMP! He had landed on the Serpent's waiting back and slid down into one of his U-bends.

As they continued their voyage towards the island, King Loofah suddenly had an idea.

"This parachute on my back ... well, if I were to stand for the remainder of this trip, the handkerchief would fill with air sideways, instead of upside down as it just did, and it would pull us along in the direction we want to go!"

Loofah stood up as near to the middle point of the Serpent's back as he could. The wind blew out the handkerchief, and made the mermaids dance and shake as though they were real and free in the ocean. Loofah watched the sky fill with stars until it sparkled above them like an enchanted city. It reminded him of home.

How King Loofah is captured by Pirates and rescued by the Serpent

Loofah and the Serpent were so busy with their own thoughts that they didn't hear the sounds of a large ship bobbing up behind them, nor did they hear the swish of a rope being thrown around the Serpent's tail, and gently tightened.

A few moments later, a small shadowy figure, followed by another, then another, then three more, crept on board the Serpent, and grabbed the unsuspecting king from behind. (Later, Loofah decided that the rude giant man had definitely done damage to his hearing, or otherwise he would surely have heard the Pirates as they sneaked up behind him.)

Poor Loofah was completely overpowered. Then he was blindfolded and his hands were roughly tied behind his back. He felt himself being dragged along the Serpent's knobbly back, up and down, up and down (the U-bends again), splosh, splosh, and then lifted up and thrown onto something hard and cold.

As bravely as he could appear, Loofah flung off the blindfold. (Now, how he did this I have never found out. I got this story from one of his people, and they heard it straight from the Palace, but Loofah would not explain how he managed it with both hands tied behind his back. We must assume that either he shook his head very hard indeed, or else he was lying.) King Loofah found himself standing face to face with a band of very fierce Pirates—blackbeards, redbeards, patch eyes, black eyes and peg legs, all with swords flashing in the moonlight.

"Well, me 'earties, what 'ave we 'ere?" spoke the ugliest Pirate, with CAPTIN written across his woolly hat. "Not much of a catch this time o' night!"

"Well, if 'e ain't got no treasure," replied another, "we can at least 'ave some fun an' make 'im walk the ol' plank!" They all laughed horribly, sending chills down Loofah's royal spine. They prodded his ribs, pulled at his furry coat and striped pyjamas, and shrieked.

"Empty yer pockets!" cried Pegleg.

"Give us yer watch!" yelled Blackbeard.

"Take off yer posh clothes!"

"Them sharks is waitin' for ya!"

Loofah was only a little afraid; he had met so many rude people recently that he felt more than capable of handling this silly band of hooligans. What they needed, he told himself, as they began to rip off his coat, was a good talking to, about manners and things. But first …

Loofah raised his hands in kingly fashion and shouted, "Now wait, everyone! Gentlemen, please listen!" The Pirates laughed and nudged each other. Captin winked, and waved everyone to be quiet.

Loofah continued. "I have an offer you cannot refuse! If you let me free, unharmed, you may become kings of all you can see from my Palace Window." What Loofah had forgotten was that he was no longer wearing his crown, and the Pirates began to laugh again and jeer at him in disbelief.

Loofah was just beginning to think that this was the beginning of the end for him when, suddenly, the ship gave a great groan and began to lean slowly over to one side, tipping Pirates and prisoner down to the other end of the deck.

A large and hideous face peered down on them, dribbling salt blobs, and blowing fishy fumes through its horrible nostrils. The Serpent had drifted over to see what was going on, and he was angry with the Pirates for stealing his king-size catch. On his head sat Loofah's second-best crown.

"Sssilly Piratesss!" he snarled and spat. "Releassse the king at onccce! I want to get going ssso I can become a king!"

The cowardly Pirates fell over each other in their rush to pull up anchor and unfurl the sails. They couldn't believe their luck. There they were, thinking they'd only caught some silly madman. But no, he really was a king and, what's more, he was going to make them kings, and share his treasure with them!

"Full steam ahead me 'earties!" sang Captin. "Er, which way, Yer Majestay?" Loofah pointed towards the misty pink horizon. The sun was just about to set on his precious island.

How King Loofah is kingnapped by the Albatross

The following day, a beautiful sea-bird flew in front of the sun, its shadow skimming over the waving blue sea. It was the Albatross, out fishing for his breakfast.

He was heading straight for a sight that interested him very much, although he could scarcely believe his eyes—a Serpent wearing a crown and a galleon full of Pirates tied to its tail. Most unusual!

The Albatross swooped down closer, gliding down on his long white wings. This time he spied the juiciest morsel he had ever set eyes upon and, goodness me, it was already cooked! King Loofah was sun-bathing on the ship's deck. As quick as a flash of lightning, the hungry bird turned into a kingnapping bird, pounced on the sizzling Loofah and carried him off into the clouds. He did this so quickly that none of the Pirates saw what had happened until it was far too late to do anything. By the time Loofah dared to open his eyes, the ship and the Serpent had become a dot and a squiggle on the ocean far below him.

Loofah was hungry, tired, sunburned and beginning to feel rather cross. He decided that the only way to handle this snooty sea-bird was to put him in his place once and for all. For hadn't he, King Loofah, recently fought off, single-handedly, Serpent, Giant, and a savage band of man-eating Pirates?

"Excuse me, young bird!" began the brave Loofah. "I don't know what your game is, but put me down now this minute!" Then, remembering where they were, he added quickly, "Er no, on second thought, don't put me down right at this minute. Let's talk this out, man to bird."

The Albatross remained silent. Loofah was just beginning to think that this must be a dumb bird, as well as a bad-mannered one, when he realised that the creature couldn't talk—his mouth was full of king! Loofah thought that, for the time being, it would be better for him if the bird did not answer. He would try out his plan on the sea-bird, but decided he would do all the talking. "By the way, dear bird, you may not have realised this, but you could become a very wealthy bird indeed."

Good. Still no response.

"If you abandon your original idea, to feed me to your babies and wife, or keep me as a slave in your nest, then I, the Great King Loofah of the Island Out at Sea, will make you king of all you can see from my Palace Window. Quite an offer, I think you'll agree."

There was no reply, but Loofah felt the beak tighten its hold, and the Albatross changed its direction. Loofah crossed his fingers and hoped that he was being taken home.

Home at last and how King Loofah keeps his promise

What seemed to Loofah like a very long time afterwards, he saw ahead of them, glistening like a jagged jewel, his precious island, covered in tall and magnificent buildings, and iced with its silver streams. He could just make out Cook, hanging out the washing, and there was the most wonderful smell of sausages wafting up to his royal nose.

He could also make out the small, distant figures of the Serpent and the Pirates, still out at sea but heading straight for the island pier, where all boats and visitors arrived. They had not forgotten Loofah's promise. They were tired and hungry, cross and grumpy, and eager for their rewards.

The Albatross began to drift downwards gently, like an autumn leaf, until at last they were circling over the tallest tower of the Royal Palace. King Loofah was home, alive and well.

"Ah yes, that will do very nicely, my friend. Just drop me off here!" shouted the happy king. "And come in for a cup of tea before the others get here."

But the Albatross was already circling upwards once more, and called out to Loofah, "No thank you, Your Majesty. As soon as I knew you were the missing King of the Island Out at Sea, I realised I must return you at once, which I have now done. But as for your offer, I have no interest in becoming a king. I have all that I need or could ever want, although you could leave a few sausages out for me each day. It would make a nice change from fish, I can tell you!" And with that, he stretched his neck and soared high into the sky, to look for dinner of a less royal kind.

King Loofah's thoughts turned to his own dinner. It was so long since he had last eaten! He'd get Cook to make extra everything. Suddenly, however, he heard a loud banging and shouting at the Palace Gates. His guests had arrived. Loofah thought dismally of how he would have to deal with them all on an empty stomach. He opened the gates himself, and there stood the band of fierce Pirates, with the Serpent slinking up behind them. He was still wearing the second-best crown, although it was now dented and green and quite tatty, Loofah noticed sadly.

"All right then, Lewfar!" growled Captin. "We 'ere is come to 'ave a quick look at the view what's through yer winder, and then be made kings of all we do see through it!" The Pirates chuckled together, and waved their daggers in the air. The Serpeant hissed with delight, covering everyone in salty spit.

Loofah tried his best to smile. "I'm so glad you could make it, gentlemen! Please follow me. There is just one window in my Palace, in the Royal Chambers. Come this way."

Loofah led them across the Banqueting Hall, down many corridors, up umpteen winding staircases, until at last they came to a door marked:

Loofah unlocked the door with a large gold key, and a moment later they all burst into the room, pushing and shoving, and trampling the smaller Pirates underfoot.

"Here you are, my friends. The Royal Window!" shouted Loofah triumphantly, acting as if he were a ring master in a circus, introducing an amazing new act.

And there it was, readers, for all to see—the Royal Window, large and wide and gleaming clean, RIGHT ABOVE THEIR HEADS, where the ceiling usually goes!

How King Loofah just about gets away with his clever idea

The Serpent slithered himself up to his full height, and pressed his disgusting face to the glass, making it all slobbery, green and wet. The Pirates jumped and clambered onto his back and onto cupboards and chests of drawers, in order to get the best possible view. Tilted heads and bulging eyes stared through the magnificent window, and the room became silent with concentration.

Loofah waited patiently. And then, suddenly, the Serpent began to tremble and grumble, then shake and splutter, and finally screech and writhe, filling the air with thick, grey smoke from his enraged nostrils.

"Ssstupid, sssilly usss! We've been tricked!" he screamed.

Captin's face darkened, partly because of the smoke, but also because he was suddenly very angry. "'E's right, me 'earties!" he yelled. "I can't see nothin' but sky, sky an' more rotten sky!"

The other Pirates began to nod their heads in agreement, and turn their dangerous looks towards Loofah who, for the time being, was completely hidden by the increasing thick mist, closing in on them all. It took them a few minutes to find him. Loofah had been expecting this and had, sensibly, climbed onto a high cupboard, out of arm's reach. The Pirates swarmed around him, and tried to grab at his feet to pull him down.

"But wait, dear fellow kings!" began Loofah. "I don't understand why you're all so cross with me."

"Oh, don't ya now!"

"Just come down 'ere, an' we'll show ya why!"

"'Course ya' don't!"

Loofah decided to ignore all these unpleasant remarks and press on. "By coming here today and looking through the Royal Window, friends, you have seen everything that is now yours!"

He smiled at the waiting faces standing below. Swords and daggers were still flashing dangerously near, so he continued quickly. "You are now the proud owners of all the sky one could want, furnished with sunbeams and moonbeams, the clouds, the stars, night and day, rain and snow, birds, butterflies—the list is endless!"

The Pirates were grumbling less loudly now, and the Serpent had stopped jumping about and covering everyone in smoke. But they still did not look very pleased.

"What about all the rest of the stuff, then?" yelled Captin. "What about all the jewels an' gold 'an stuff? That's what kings is s'pose to 'ave, innit, not all this sky rubbish."

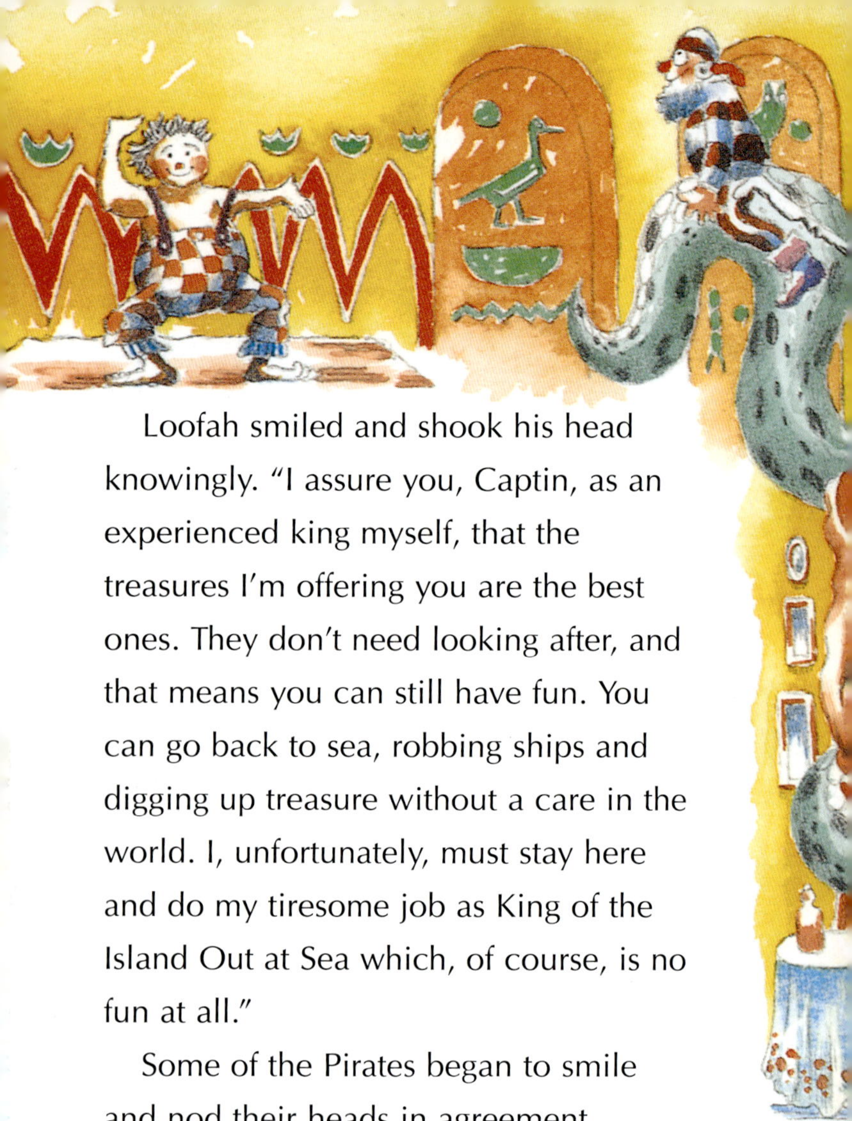

Loofah smiled and shook his head knowingly. "I assure you, Captin, as an experienced king myself, that the treasures I'm offering you are the best ones. They don't need looking after, and that means you can still have fun. You can go back to sea, robbing ships and digging up treasure without a care in the world. I, unfortunately, must stay here and do my tiresome job as King of the Island Out at Sea which, of course, is no fun at all."

Some of the Pirates began to smile and nod their heads in agreement.

"But what about our crowns?" one of them shouted.

"I have not forgotten them," Loofah replied craftily. "My servants are, at this very moment, filling your ship with golden crowns—beautiful, glistening, golden crowns."

Pirate eyes lit up around the room and the Serpent began to quiver and slobber, and to slide his way sneakily towards the bedroom door.

"And, for our dear friend Serpent," Loofah continued quickly, "there is a very special reward." Serpent turned, and pretended that he hadn't been going anywhere. "After all, if it hadn't been for his quick thinking in that terrible storm, I might easily have ended up on the bottom of the ocean!" Serpent puffed out his chest proudly, and swayed his head in agreement.

Loofah then turned to Captin. "With all that wonderful gold on board your ship, it is important that you are protected, and for that reason I have decided to appoint Serpent, Keeper of the Crowns. Wherever you go, he will be there to keep you out of trouble—er, I mean danger!"

There was loud applause and cheering from various corners of the room, and then the excited Pirates, led by their new bodyguard, charged through the Palace, and out of the gates, down to the sea where their ship awaited them. Loofah smiled wearily, and then gave orders for lunch to be served—an ENORMOUS lunch, he told Cook.

The end

"Three cheers for King Loofah!" shouted the Pirates as they paraded around the ship's deck in their new crowns.

"Hip hip hooray! Hip hip hooray! Hip hip hooray!"

"And now three cheers for King Captin! Hip hip hooray! Hip hip hooray! Hip hip hooray!"

"And now three cheers for King Pegleg! Hip hip hooray! Hip hip hoo..."

There were many new kings that night and, in the Royal Chambers, as tired King Loofah drifted off to sleep, he could hear the cheering fade away over the horizon —"... three cheers for King Blackbeard. Hip hip hooray!"

At last King Loofah was deep into his dreams, and somewhere, far out at sea, a band of happy Pirates and a Sea-Serpent hung up their crowns and also dreamed—of exciting adventures and dreadful deeds yet to come.